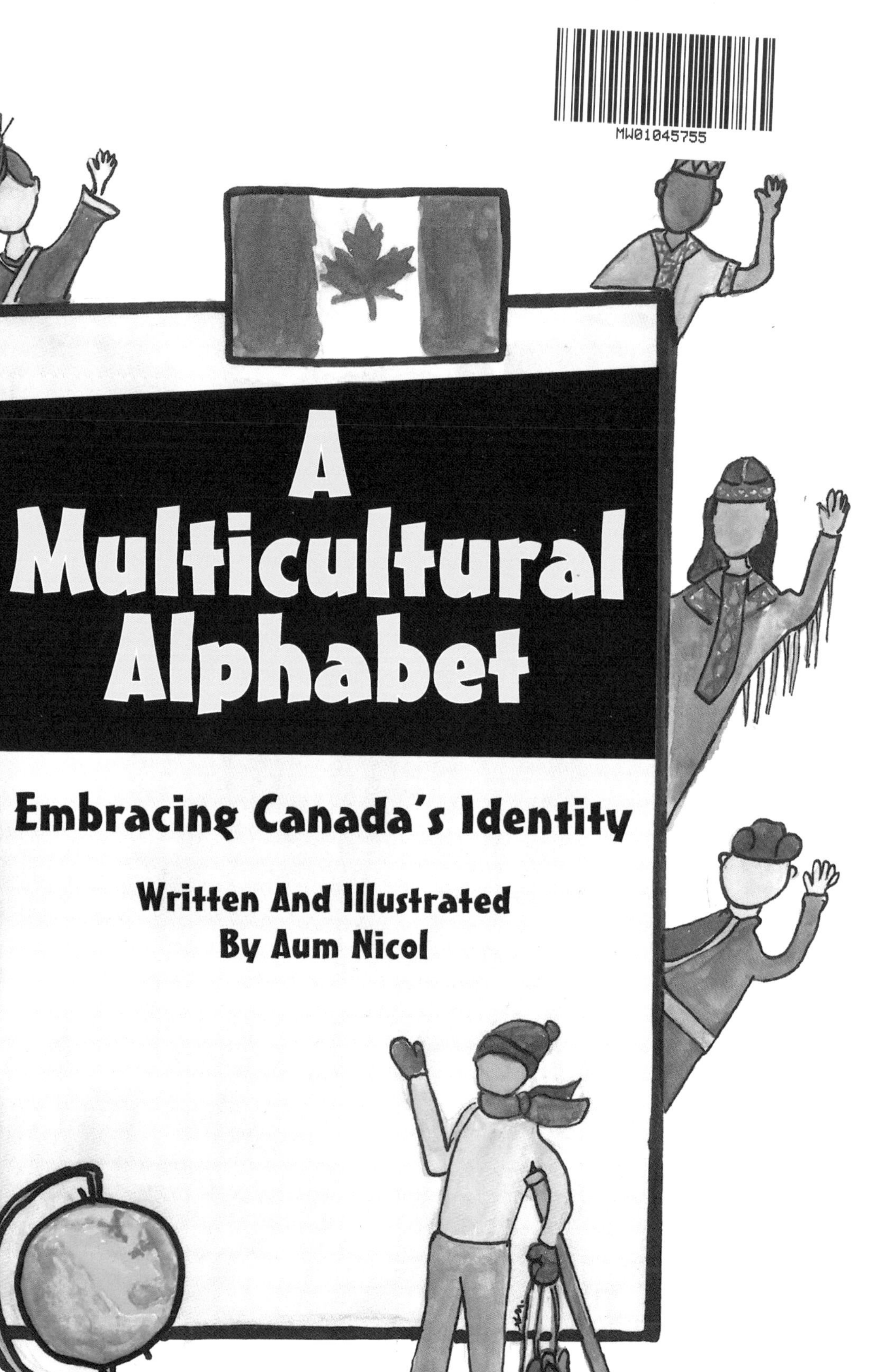

A Multicultural Alphabet

Embracing Canada's Identity

Written And Illustrated
By Aum Nicol

First Edition – July 2013

ISBN
978-1-4602-1364-3 (Paperback)
978-1-4602-1365-0 (eBook)

Produced by:

FriesenPress
Suite 300 – 852 Fort Street
Victoria, BC, Canada V8W 1H8

www.friesenpress.com

Distributed to the trade by The Ingram Book Company

To Chris,
My husband, my knight,
Thank-you for believing in me
I love you!

For all Canadians who
celebrate and respect
cultural diversity.

A is for Ancestry. All Canadians have family members who originally came from another country.

- Aboriginal
- Acadians
- Alberta
- Anne of Green Gables
- Arctic
- Atlantic Ocean
- Asian
- Aurora Borealis

is for Bilingual. Canada's official languages are English and French.

- Banff
- Bannock
- Basketball
- Bay of Fundy
- Beaver
- Bison
- Blue Nose
- Bonhomme
- Bonspiel
- British Columbia

C is for Culture. Culture is created from traditions, songs, dances, stories, beliefs, rituals, food or clothing. Canada is a nation of people who have brought their cultures from other countries.

- Calgary Stampede
- Canada Goose
- Canadian Shield
- Canoe
- Cape Breton
- Caribou
- Celsius
- Charlottetown
- Chinook
- Confederation

is for Diversity. Canada accepts and respects people from different races and cultures. Diversity provides variety and opportunities!

- Dawson City
- Dinosaur
- Celine Dion
- Dog Sled
- Drumheller

E is for English. In 1497, John Cabot (Giovanni Caboto) claimed Newfoundland and Cape Breton Island for England.

- Edmonton
- Eh?
- Ethnicity
- Evergreen

F is for French. In 1534, Jacques Cartier sailed from France. In 1541 he began to create a settlement where Quebec City is now located.

- First Nations
- Fleur-de-lis
- Forests
- Flurries
- Terry Fox
- Fredricton
- Fishermen

G is for Government. Canadians live in a democratic society which means people can vote for their leaders.

- Chief Dan George
- Gaspe Penninsula
- Great Lakes
- Grizzly Bear
- Nancy Greene
- Wayne Gretzky

H is for Heritage Festivals. All across Canada there are summer festivals where many cultures are celebrated with food and dance!

- Gordie Howe
- Habitant
- Halifax
- Hockey
- Homesteaders
- Hudson's Bay
- Humpback Whales
- Husky

I is for Indigenous People. First Nations People lived in communities before Europeans came to Canada. They are: The Inuit, Iroquois, Plains, Plateau and Coastal People

- Ice
- Iceberg
- Icicles
- Igloo
- IMAX
- Immigrant
- Insulin
- Inukshuk
- Inuvik
- Iqaluit

J is for Justice.

Canadians are protected by laws to ensure they all have fair and reasonable treatment.

- Jasper
- Jays
- John Deere
- July 1st, 1867
- Juniper
- Juno Awards

A.N.

K is for Kanata. Kanata is the Aboriginal word for “village” or “land”. Kanata became Canada.

- Kayak
- Killerwhale
- Klondike
- Komatik
- Kookum

L is for Land. Canada has two mountain ranges and borders on three oceans. The land has a variety of geographical features such as: fjords, tundra, permafrost, prairies, swamps, bogs and lakes.

- Labrador
- Lacrosse
- Lakes
- Lighthouse
- Lobster
- Loon
- Lumberjack
- Wilfred Laurier

is for Mosaic. Canada is a beautiful mosaic of unique cultures, races, languages and traditions.

- John A. MacDonald
- Mallard Duck
- Manitoba
- Maple Leaf
- Maritimes
- Metis
- Mining
- Moose
- Mooshum
- Mosquito
- Mountie
- Muskeg

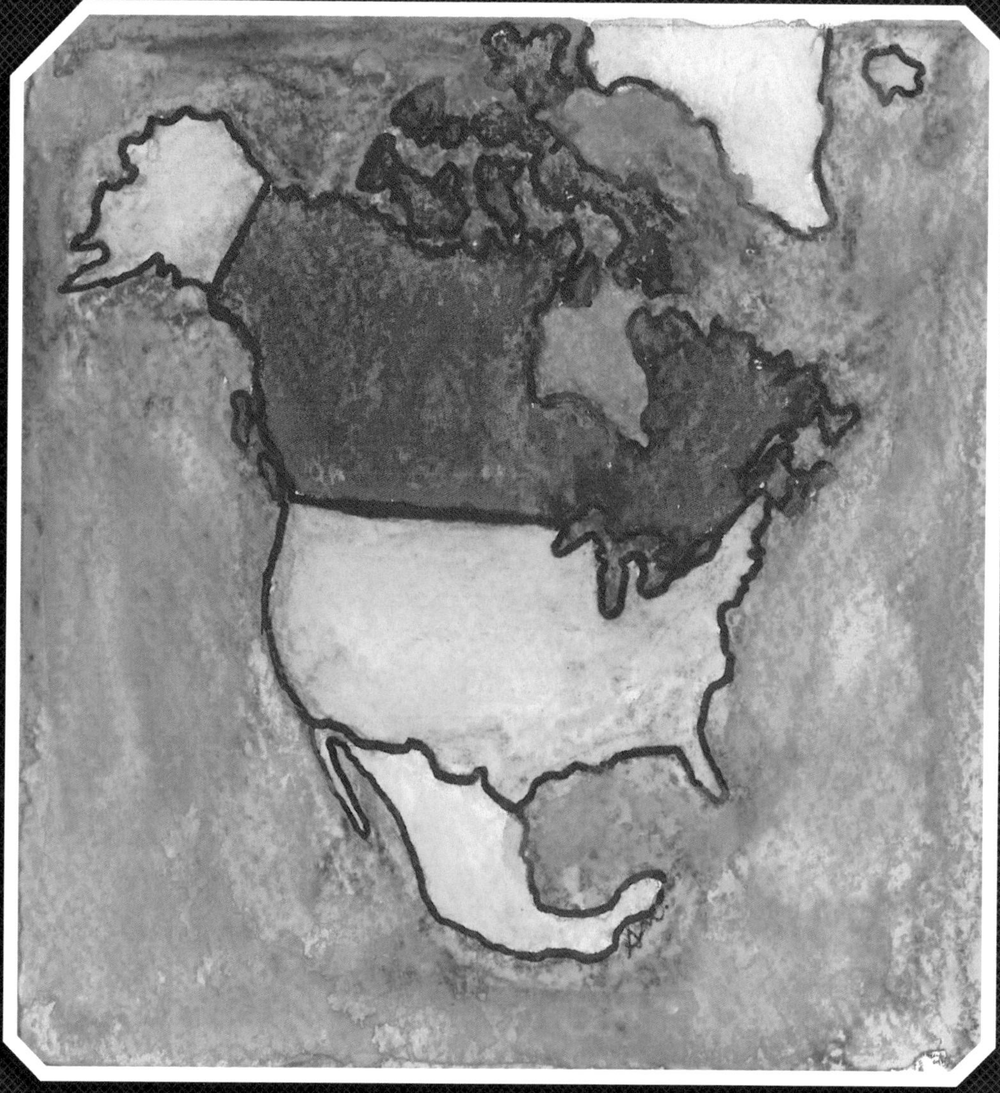

N is for North. Canada starts at 49° N and reaches into the Arctic Ocean.

- New Brunswick
- Newfoundland
- Niagara Falls
- Nickel
- Norse
- Northwest Territories
- Nova Scotia
- Nunavet

O is for Opportunity. Canada's land offered early settlers a new life. Today, there are many opportunities for people to live, work and play.

- Ontario
- Ottawa
- Ogopogo
- Bobby Orr
- Oil

P is for Parliament. Each province is governed by a premier who goes to parliament to work with the Prime Minister. Parliament is in Ottawa.

- Lester B. Pearson
- Pacific Ocean
- Pier 21
- Pioneers
- Polar Bears
- Potlatch
- Poutine
- Prairie
- Prince Edward Island

is for Queen. Queen Elizabeth II became Head of State for Canada in 1952.

- Quahog
- Quarter Horse
- Qu' Appelle
- Quebec
- Quebec City
- Queque

R is for Rights and Responsibilities. The Charter of Rights and Responsibilities ensures all people will be treated with respect. It is the responsibility of Canadians to treat others with respect.

- Louis Reil
- Railway
- Regina
- Remembrance Day
- Rockies
- Rodeo
- Royal Canadian Mounted Police

is for Society. A multicultural society allows people to dress, work, and follow their customs and languages without fear of being treated disrespectfully.

- Saskatchewan
- Salmon
- Santa Claus
- Skates
- Snow
- Snowshoes
- St. John's
- Stanley Park

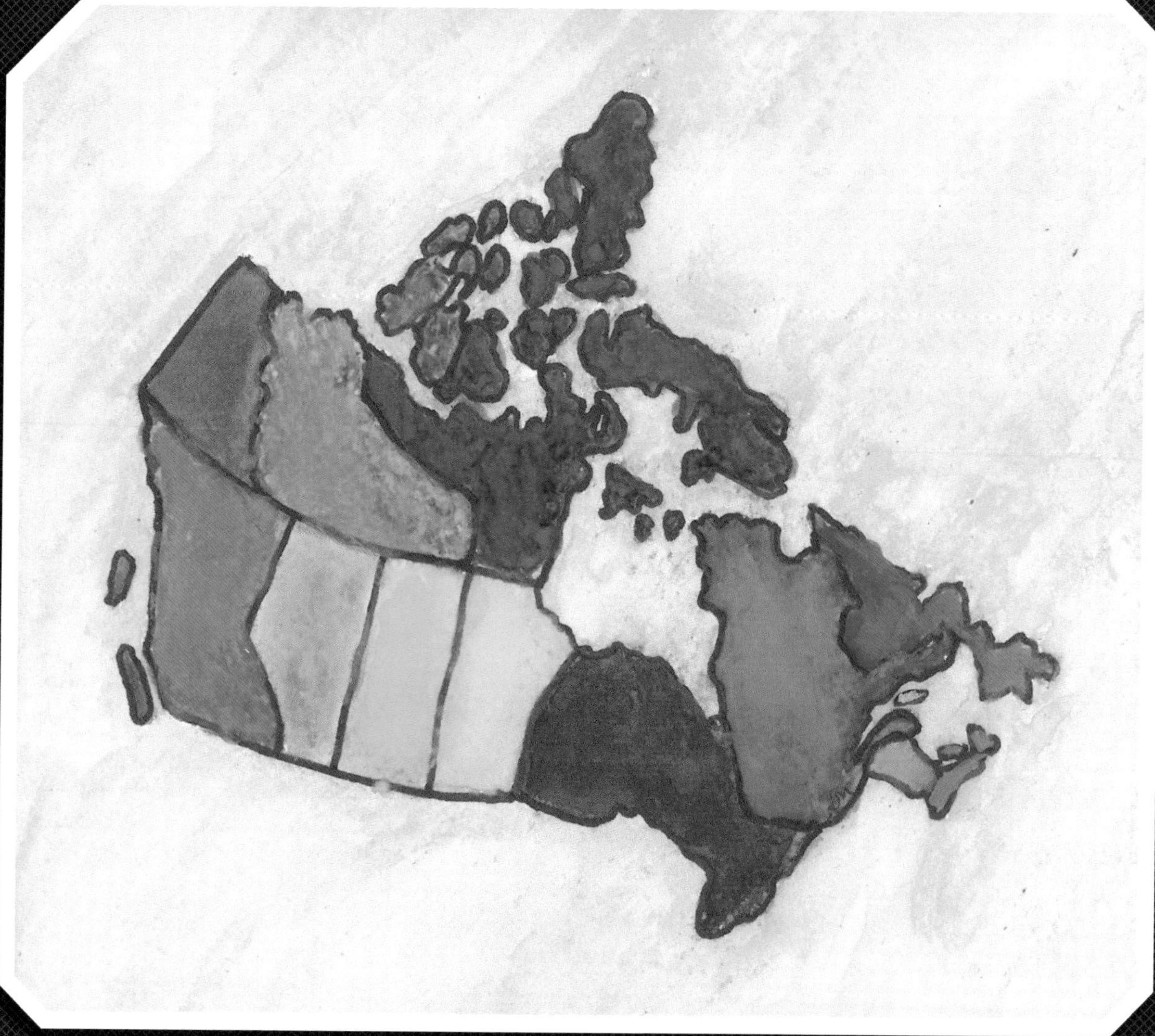

T is for Ten Provinces and Three Territories.

- Tortière
- Tar Sands
- Tim Hortons
- Toboggan
- Toronto
- Totem Pole
- TransCanada Highway
- Treaties
- Pierre Elliott Trudeau

U

is for Unity. Canadians stand together during good times and times of need.

- Ulu
- Umiyak
- Ungava Bay
- United Empire Loyalists
- Uranium

V is for Vikings. Vikings settled in Canada in 1000 AD. Leif Erikson was the first visitor from Europe.

- Vancouver Island
- Vancouver
- Victoria
- Voyageurs

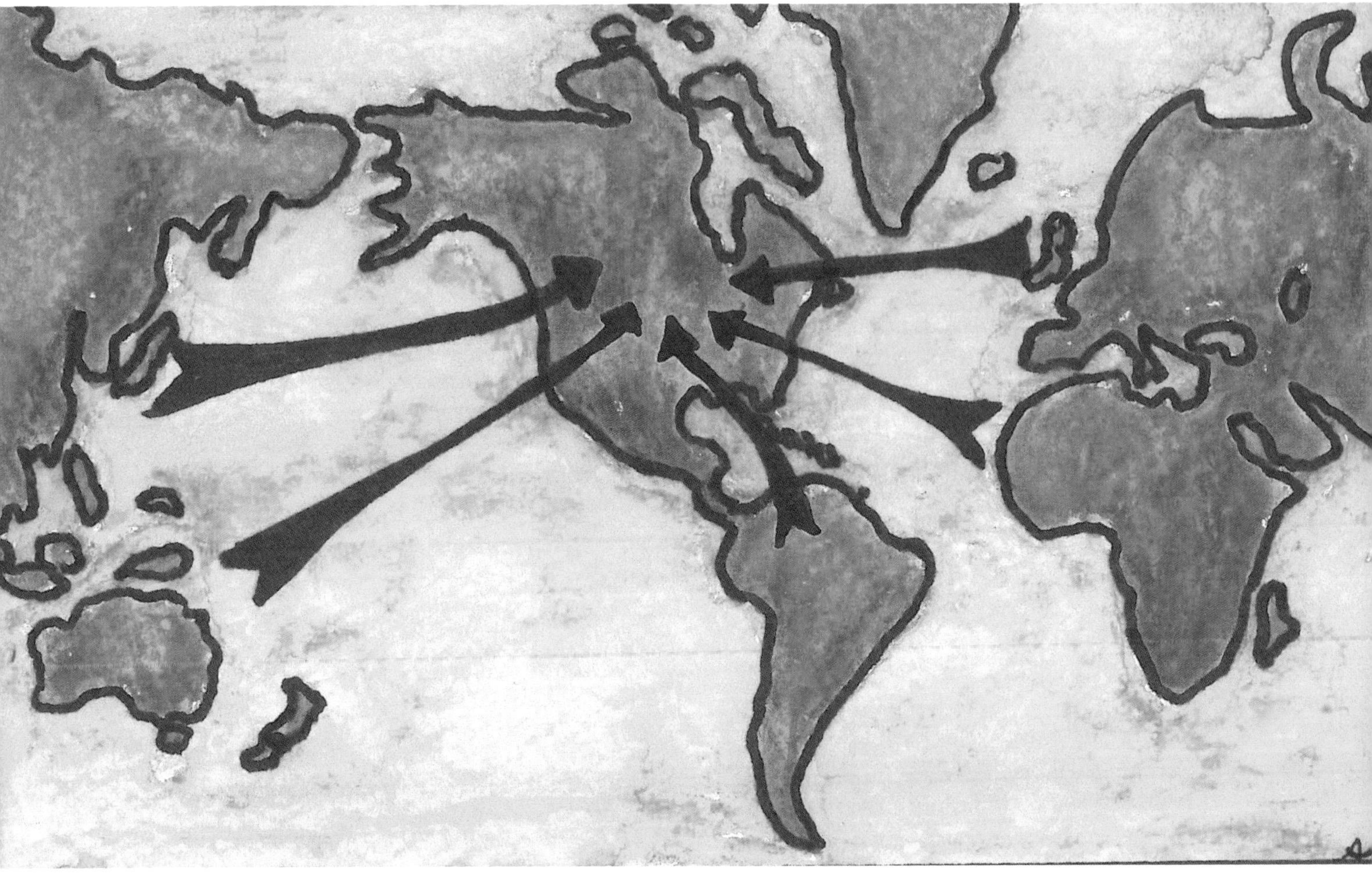

W is for World. We have representatives from the whole world in one country!

- Waxwing
- Wheat
- Whitehorse
- Winnipeg
- Winter
- Wolf

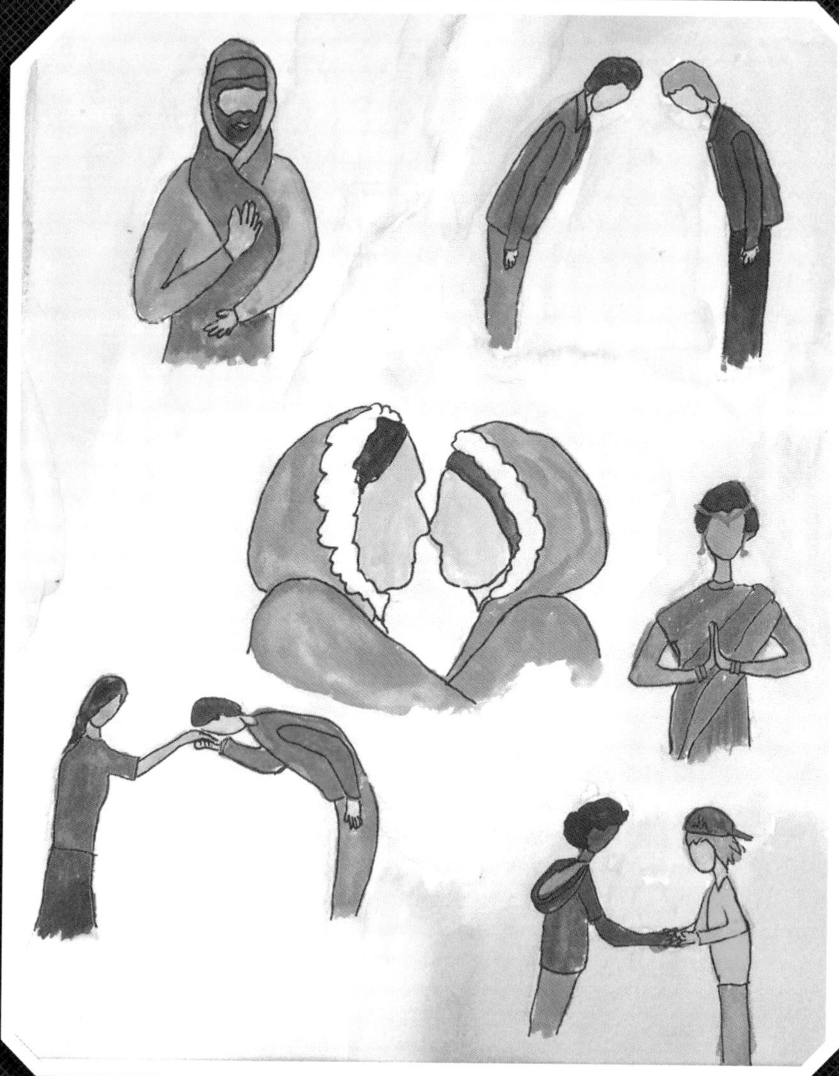

X is for X-Cultural. Cross-Cultural awareness allows us to find ways to communicate with people of different backgrounds and traditions.

- Xenon Gas
- X-Country

Y is for Youth! Young Canadians hold the future. Each generation must ensure that all of Canada's many cultures are respected and celebrated!

- Yarmouth
- Yellowhead Pass
- Yellowknife
- Yoho National Park
- Yukon

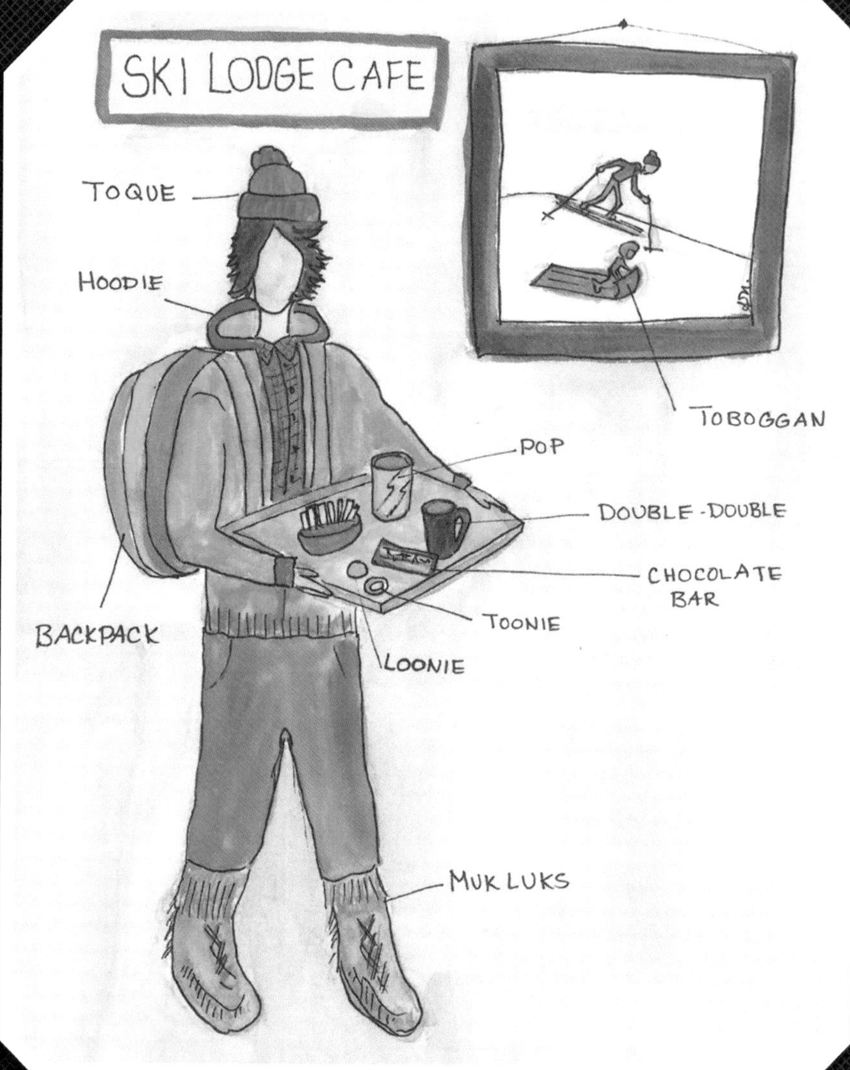

Z is for the letter Zed and the many Zany words Canadians have for everyday things.

- Zamboni
- Zed
- Zellers
- Zinc
- Zipper

Glossary

A

Aboriginal:	people who lived in Canada from the earliest times
Acadians:	French settlers in the Maritimes
Alberta:	a western prairie province
Anne of Green Gables:	a novel by Canadian author Lucy Maud Montgomery from 1908
Arctic:	the area around the North Pole
Atlantic Ocean:	the ocean on Canada's eastern coast
Asian:	someone whose ancestry was from the continent of Asia
Aurora: Borealis	northern lights

B

Banff:	a town in the Rocky Mountains
Bannock:	a round, flat bread cooked over a fire by the aboriginals
Basketball:	this game was invented in 1891 by Canadian, James Naismith
Bay of Fundy	a body of water 270 kilometres long with the highest tides in the world
Beaver:	national symbol of Canada; its fur was traded by the Hudson's Bay Company
Bison or Buffalo:	millions used to roam the Great Plains
Bluenose:	a famous schooner from Nova Scotia, the symbol is on the back of the ten cent coin
Bonhomme:	snowman mascot for Quebec's Winter Carnival
Bonspiel:	a tournament for the game of curling
British Columbia:	Canada's west coast province

C

Calgary Stampede:	an annual rodeo in Calgary
Canada Goose:	a wild goose that migrate to southern U.S and Mexico returning to Canada in the spring in V-formations
Canadian Shield;	a large area in central Canada of Precambrian rock rich in minerals
Canoe:	a lightweight boat made by Indigenous people of North America
Cape Breton:	an island on the north eastern part of Nova Scotia
Caribou:	part of the deer family; on the back of the Canadian 25 cent coin
Celsius:	the unit of measurement for temperature in Canada
Charlottetown:	capital city of Prince Edward Island
Chinook:	a warm wind blowing down the eastern slopes of the Rockies
Confederation:	Ontario, Quebec, New Brunswick, Nova Scotia became the Dominion of Canada on July 1st, 1867

D

Dawson City:	a town in the Yukon at the heart of the Klondike Gold Rush
Dinosaur:	many of the ancient reptile bones are found near Drumheller and Grande Prairie, Alberta
Celine Dion:	award winning Canadian singer from Quebec
Dog Sled:	a sled pulled by a team of dogs in the Arctic
Drumheller:	town in southern Alberta famous for their deposit of dinosaur bones

E

Edmonton:	capital city of Alberta

Eh?: (ay) a popular expression in Canada, "How's it goin', eh?"

Ethnicity: a person's race, religious, linguistic, national or cultural background

Evergreen: a tree that stays green throughout the year

F

First Nations: Aboriginal people of Canada but not Metis nor Inuit

Fleur-de lis a lily or iris used as a symbol on Quebec's provincial flag and Canadian coat of arms

Forests: Canada has 1.4 billion acres of forest

Flurries: wind and light snow

Terry Fox: Canadian hero who attempted to run across Canada in 1980 with one leg for Cancer research

Fredericton: Capital city of New Brunswick

Fishermen: Canada's east and west coasts abundant fish population created this job until over fishing occurred

G

Chief Dan George: a famous chief of a Coast Salish band in British Columbia. He was an author, poet and actor

Gaspe Peninsula: land that juts out into the Gulf of St. Lawrence River

Great Lakes: 5 large freshwater lakes shared by Canada and United states

Grizzly Bear: Canada's second largest carnivore

Nancy Greene: Canada's champion alpine skier

Wayne Gretzky: "Great One" is one of Canada's famous professional hockey player

Gold Rush: a time during 1896-1899 where prospectors searched for gold in Canada's Yukon

H

Habitant:	French settlers along the St. Lawrence River
Halifax:	Capital city of Nova Scotia
Hockey:	one of Canada's national sports using curved sticks, a puck, skates and ice
Homesteaders:	people who came from other countries to own and work land to populate Canada
Hudson's Bay:	a large body of water in northeastern Canada named after English explorer Henry Hudson
Hudson's Bay Company:	began as a fur trading post used to exchange furs from the Natives for knives, pots, beads and other items.
Humpback Whales:	the world's fifth largest whale can be found on Canada`s east and west coast
Husky:	a dog used to pull sleds in northern Canada

I

Ice:	frozen water of which Canada has plenty
Iceberg:	a massive piece of floating ice broken from a glacier; can be seen off the Newfoundland coast in spring
Icicles:	a triangular spike of ice formed when water melts and freezes
Igloo:	an Inuit home of the past in the shape of a dome built with blocks of hard snow
IMAX:	a large screen movie format created by a Canadian company
Immigrant:	a person who has moved into a new country in order to resettle
Insulin:	a protein hormone that lowers blood sugar discovered by Canadian scientists, Fredrick G. Banting, Charles H. Best, J.J.R. Macleod and James B. Collip. Insulin helps those with diabetes all around the world.
Inukshuk:	a stone figure built by Inuit for hunting, directions or messages
Inuvik:	a town in the Northwest Territories

Iqaluit: capital city of Nunavut

J

Jasper: a city in the Rocky Mountains; a great tourist and vacation spot

Jays: a species of bird that lives permanently in Canada: Blue Jay, Stellar Jay and the Gray Jay

July 1st, 1867: the day in which the Dominion of Canada was formed

Juniper: a hardy needle-like shrub found in Canada

Juno Awards: Canada`s Academy of Recording Arts and Sciences celebrating Canadian Music.

K

Kayak: a lightweight canoe used by the Inuit that has small opening for the paddler to sit in

Killerwhale: a black and white sharp-toothed whale found on Canada`s west coast and Arctic ocean

Klondike: an area in the Yukon where gold was discovered in 1896 causing the gold rush

Komatik: a dog sled used by the Inuit to travel in winter

Kookum: Cree word for Grandmother

L

Labrador: a region of eastern Canada that is part of Newfoundland

Lacrosse: a First Nations game played with a netted stick and ball; Canada`s national sport

Lakes: a lake is a large body of water surrounded by land. As large ice shields, called glaciers, melted, they formed over 30,000 lakes in Canada.

Lighthouse: a tower that uses a beacon of light to warn ships of the coastline

Lobster Industry: the large edible crustacean is harvested for their meat. Canada supplies over half the world's demands for lobster!

Loon: a black throated, aquatic bird found on many of Canada's lakes; it is the symbol on the back of Canada's one dollar coin and is the reason it is nicknamed the "Loonie"

Lumberjack: a woodcutter or logger found in Canada's vast forest areas, cutting and transporting wood to sawmills

Wilfred Laurier: Canada's first French prime minister

M

John A. MacDonald: Canada's first Prime Minister

Mallard Duck: found in Canada; the males have a bright green head while females are speckled brown

Manitoba: one of the prairie provinces between Saskatchewan and Ontario.

Maple Leaf: symbol of Canada since the early 1700s

Maritimes: Canada's east coast provinces: New Brunswick, Nova Scotia, Prince Edward Island

Metis: are Aboriginal people whose ancestors were mixed First Nations and Europeans

Mining: Canada has a history of mining important minerals found all over but has rich deposits in the Canadian Shield such as nickel, gold, silver, copper, zinc

Moose: member of the deer family found in Canada with long legs and large antlers; it is the symbol on the back of the twenty-five cent coin

Mooshum: Cree name for Grandfather

Mountie: short for the Royal Canadian Mounted Police

Muskeg: a type of bog or wetland with peat or moss found in northern and western Canada

N

Native: the name used to identify the Indigenous people of Canada; someone born of a specific area

New Brunswick: a Maritime province

Newfoundland: Canada's easternmost Atlantic province

Niagara Falls: world famous waterfalls on the Canadian and U.S. border

Nickel: a greyish-white metallic element found in soil and rock; it is also the name of the Canadian five cent coin

Norse: Scandinavian people such as the Vikings whose buildings have been found dating 1000 AD

Northwest Territories: one of Canada's northern territories located between the Yukon and Nunavut

Nova Scotia: a maritime province

Nunavut: the largest northern territory

O

Ontario: a province in central Canada

Ottawa: Nation's capital

Ogopogo: a Salish name for a legendary lake monster considered to live in Okanagan Lake

Bobby Orr: a famous Canadian hockey player

Oil: Canada's oil sands found near Fort McMurray supply Canada, United States and the world with petroleum

P

Pacific Ocean: the ocean found on Canada's west coast

Pier 21: a terminal in Halifax for ocean liners bringing immigrants to Canada from Europe from 1928-1971

Pioneers:	Europeans who were the first to explore and settle parts of Canada
Polar Bears:	a white furred bear found in the Arctic and Canada's largest land predator
Potlatch:	a ceremony among First Nations people where gifts are distributed
Poutine:	a Quebec dish of French fries topped with gravy and curd cheese
Prairie:	a treeless area of flat grassy land that has fertile soil used for growing grain
Prince Edward Island:	the smallest province in Canada located in the Gulf of St. Lawrence

Q

Quahog:	the Algonquin name for a large clam-like mollusk found on Canada's East Coast
Quarter Horse:	a breed of horse that were a favorite to Canadian farmers from the 1920s
Qu' Appelle:	a small village in Saskatchewan
Quebec:	Canada's mainly French-speaking east-central province
Quebec City:	the capital of Quebec
Louis Reil:	folk hero the leader of the Metis people on the Canadian prairies who sought to protect their rights and culture

R

Railway:	the Canadian Pacific Railway unites Canada from coast to coast
Regina:	Capital city of Saskatchewan

Remembrance Day: the day set aside to commemorate the end of World War 1 and those in the armed forces who have died in the line of duty. Canadians wear a red poppy in memory of the war dead.

Rockies: the nickname for the Rocky Mountains in western Canada

Rodeo: a sporting event that involves cowboys or cowgirls, horses and livestock. It includes such events as roping, steer wrestling, bull riding, chuck wagon racing and barrel racing

Royal Canadian Mounted Police: also known as the RCMP; the federal and national police force of Canada founded in 1873

S

Saskatchewan: one of Canada's prairie provinces

Salmon: a species of fish that grow in the ocean then migrate upstream into Canadian fresh water rivers and lakes in order to reproduce.

Santa Claus: considered to live in the Arctic

Skates: boots with blades used to glide on ice

Snow: small ice crystals formed from water

Snowshoes: a light frame with laces for boots used to walk on top of snow

St. John's: captial city of Newfoundland

Stanley Park: a beautiful natural park in Vancouver, BC

T

Tortière: a meat pie from Quebec traditionally served at Christmas.

Tar Sands: the Athabasca oil sands in Alberta are loose sand, clay and water containing petroleum

Tim Hortons:	a professional hockey player opened a doughnut coffee shop in 1964 and is now Canada's largest fast food service
Toboggan:	a long narrow sled for sliding downhill
Toronto:	capital of Ontario
Totem Pole:	a tall cedar tree that is carved with images made by the Coastal Natives
TransCanada Highway:	a highway that joins all ten provinces
Treaties:	a negotiation to reach an agreement
Pierre Elliott Trudeau:	Canada's 15th Prime Minister who established the Charter of Rights and Freedoms and introduced Canada's 'Multiculturalism Policy' in 1971

U

Ulu:	an Inuit knife having a short curved blade with the handle on the top.
Umiak:	a boat used by the Inuit
Ungava Bay:	an oval body of water on Quebec's northern coastline; name means "Far Away"
United Empire Loyalists:	people who left during the American Revolution and settled in Canada
Uranium:	a heavy metal that is mined in Canada and used in nuclear energy

V

Vancouver Island:	a large island on Canada's west coast
Vancouver:	the largest city on British Columbia's coast
Victoria:	the capital city of British Columbia
Voyageurs:	woodsmen, boatmen, trappers and guides for Canada's fur trading company

W

Waxwing: a songbird found in Canada

Wheat: a popular grain grown in Canada used to make cereals and flour

Whitehorse: capital of Yukon Territories

Winnipeg: capital of Manitoba

Winter: the coldest season of the year

Wolf: a wild member of the dog family living in Canada's northern areas

X

Xenon Gas: a gas used as a beacon in Canada's lighthouses

X-Country Skiing: Norwegian-Canadian Herman Smith Johannsen introduced cross-country skiing to Canada

Y

Yarmouth: means "Land's End" in Mi'kmaq and is a small town in southern Nova Scotia

Yellowhead Pass: is a mountain pass in the Rockies going across the continental divide between Alberta and British Columbia

Yellowknife: capital of Northwest Territories

Yoho National Park: Yoho is the Cree word for expressing awe. Yoho National Park is in southwestern British Columbia

Yukon: the westernmost northern territory

Z

Zamboni: a riding machine that cleans the ice at skating and hockey rinks

Zed: the name Canadians use for the last letter of the alphabet

Zellers: a discount store founded in 1931 and part of the Hudson's Bay now sold to the Target company

Zinc: Canada is the largest producer of this blue-white metal

Zipper: Gideon Sundback invented the modern zipper used as a closure on most clothing

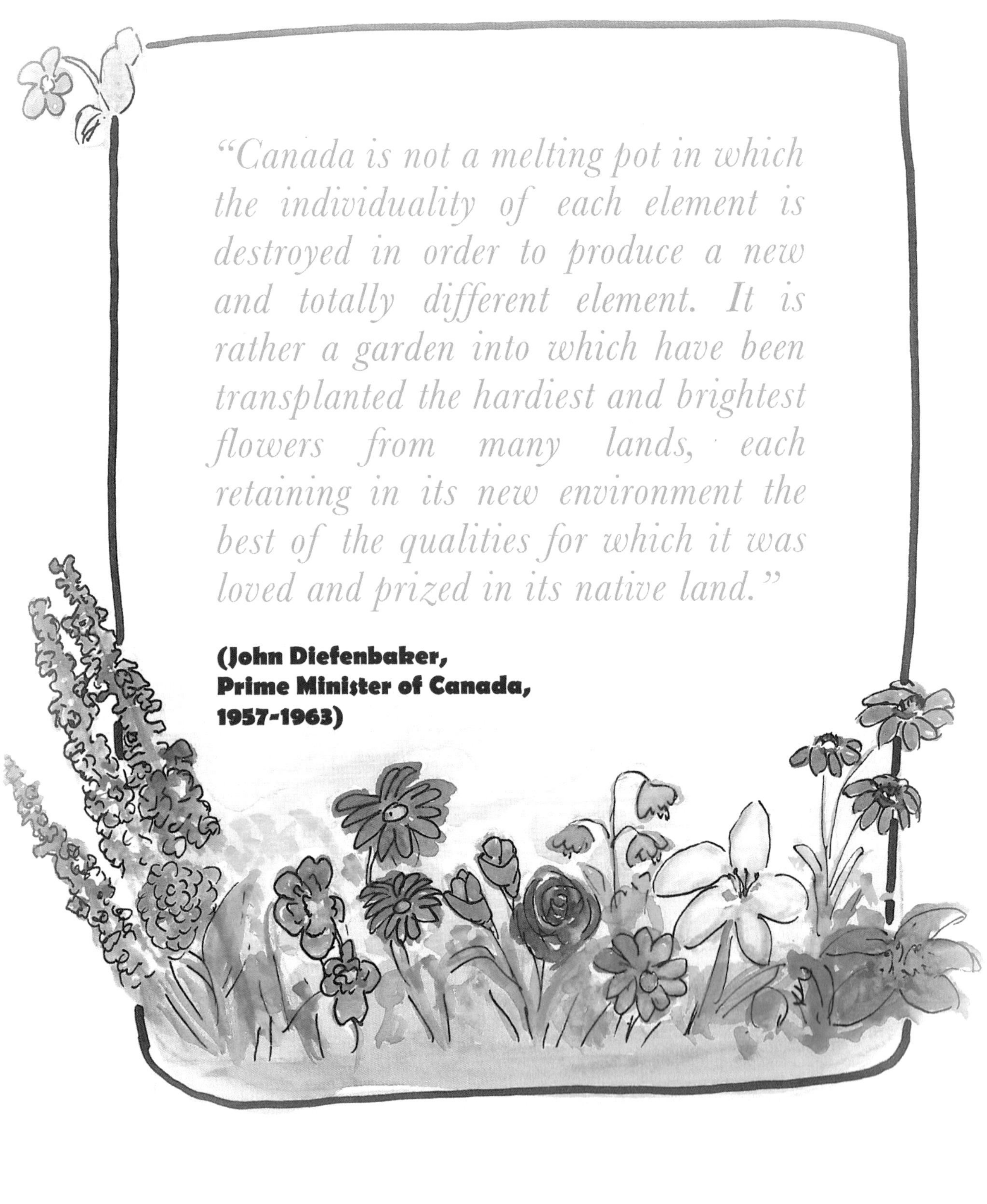

"Canada is not a melting pot in which the individuality of each element is destroyed in order to produce a new and totally different element. It is rather a garden into which have been transplanted the hardiest and brightest flowers from many lands, each retaining in its new environment the best of the qualities for which it was loved and prized in its native land."

(John Diefenbaker, Prime Minister of Canada, 1957-1963)

Acknowledgements

This project has been 5 years in the making even though the idea was conceived 20 years ago. I started by looking up terms in the Multicultural Act of Canada and setting them to rhyme. It was the worst piece of writing I ever did!! After encouragement from my husband, I narrowed my focus to create the simpler style in this book. It was Chris' love, encouragement and total belief in me that enabled me to work on my illustrations through the pain and fatigue associated with chemotherapy and radiation treatments for Breast Cancer. I cannot thank him enough!

To the following friends and family, you willingly joined me on this dream and without your help and guidance, I could not have completed this work. My love and gratitude go out to you!!

Support Team: Chris Nicol, Alyssa Nicol, Josh Nicol, Wilena Nicol, Anjanee Gyan-Dyck, Atma Persad, Sita Gorski, Kim Lock, Barb Roth, Vanessa Mungal, Linda Williams

Editing: Dave and Christine Jones

Creative Consulting: Chris Nicol, Anu Sharma, Hilary Gray, Jan Hoffart, Lorraine Robinson, John and Rita Murray

I also want to dedicate this book to Westlock Elementary School. I grew as a teacher from the example and support from my colleagues and administrators (1989-2002) Westlock, Alberta

To the staff and parents of the Little School With So Much Heart-St. Clement School in Grande Prairie, Alberta.

CPSIA information can be obtained
at www.ICGtesting.com
Printed in the USA
LVIC01n1434161113
361588LV00012BA/132
9781460213643